Praise For

Faith in the Fog

I liked that Charlotte includes a tool to replace lies readers are believing with truth. Many times, you just have to choose to believe the truth when you don't feel it. It looks like a good supplement to go with counseling. I can see using this as homework for a Counselee.
—**Mettra Prouty**, *Biblical Counselor*

***

This workbook is amazing. Charlotte's conversational writing style drew me in and it felt like I was having a conversation with her. The workbook seamlessly blends Charlotte's story, interactive tools, and scripture reflections to offer a holistic approach to healing from trauma.
—**Krystl Michalek**, *Pastor/ Educator/Biblical Counselor*

***

The tools in this workbook, paired with Charlotte's notes, scriptures, and reflections are engaging and keep me moving forward. They give me something concrete to hang on to.
—**Mentee**

***

Having worked closely with Charlotte Thomason over the past year, I can attest to the profound impact her approach has had on my life and personal growth. Charlotte's methodology beautifully combines two essential elements often overlooked in our fast-paced world: the gift of time and the unwavering foundation of God's Word. Rather than offering quick fixes or surface-level solutions, she creates space for genuine transformation to unfold naturally, always grounding her guidance in biblical truth. Through applying the principles Charlotte outlines in this book, I've experienced meaningful change in areas where I've long struggled, discovering that lasting healing requires both patience with the process and complete trust in the wisdom found in Scripture. Charlotte's gentle yet profound approach reminds us that God's timing and His Word are sufficient for every challenge we face, and this book is an invaluable resource for anyone seeking authentic, faith-centered growth.
—**Jennifer Orenstein**, *Pastor/Business Owner*

***

Charlotte's mentorship has been a beacon of hope in my healing journey. Her unwavering guidance inspired me to heal from childhood trauma, trust myself, and deepen my faith. She has truly paved the way for my transformation. Everyone who engages with this workbook will be inspired by her courage, wisdom, and unshakeable faith, igniting their own path to healing and growth.
—**Theresa Alexander**, *HS-BCP/Doctoral Candidate*

Faith In The Fog

A Workbook For Healing When the Path Isn't Clear

Inspired by What Kind of Love Is This? Finding God in the Darkness

Charlotte B. Thomason

Published by KHARIS PUBLISHING, an imprint of KHARIS MEDIA LLC.
Copyright © 2025 Charlotte B. Thomason
ISBN-13: 978-1-63746-410-6
ISBN-10: 11-63746-410-X
Library of Congress Control Number:
All rights reserved. This book or parts thereof may not be reproduced in any form, stored in a retrieval system, or transmitted in any form by any means - electronic, mechanical, photocopy, recording, or otherwise - without prior written permission of the publisher, except as provided by United States of America copyright law.
Scripture quotations taken from The Holy Bible, New International Version®, NIV®. Copyright © 1973, 1978, 1984, 2011 by Biblica, Inc. Used with permission of Zondervan. All rights reserved worldwide
www.zondervan.com
Portions of the *Relate Journal* tool are used with permission from The Mosaic Life Network (© 2016). Adapted with acknowledgment and gratitude.
Printed in the United States of America
First Edition; www.charlottethomason.com
All KHARIS PUBLISHING products are available at special quantity discounts for bulk purchases for sales promotions, premiums, fund-raising, and educational needs. For details, contact:
Kharis Media LLC
Tel: 1-630-909-3405
support@kharispublishing.com
www.kharispublishing.com

Disclaimer

This workbook is not a substitute for counseling, therapy, or crisis support. It was created as a reflective, faith-rooted tool to support survivors and those walking alongside them.

If you find yourself feeling overwhelmed or triggered at any point, please pause and take care of yourself. Use one of the grounding tools in the workbook, talk to someone you trust, or seek help from a licensed mental health provider. If you are in crisis, contact a professional or support service in your area.

You are not alone and you don't have to walk this journey without help.

Author's Note

This workbook was born out of my healing journey, a path shaped by silence, survival, faith, and the slow work of learning to feel again. If you've walked through trauma, carried the weight of shame, or wondered where God was in the middle of it all, you are not alone.

'What Kind of Love Is This?' tells my story, but this workbook is about yours. It's designed to help you reflect on your own experiences, notice old patterns, and try out tools that gently support healing. Some come from the world of trauma recovery. Others come from faith. Together, they've helped me take one step at a time and I hope they'll do the same for you.

You don't need to read the memoir to begin. Just come as you are.

This isn't a workbook you "complete." It's one you live with. You'll find reflections, grounding tools, faith prompts, and gentle invitations, not to get it all right, but to stay curious and honest. There's room here for grace, for questions, and for starting over as many times as you need.

Thank you for trusting me to walk this road with you.

—Charlotte.

Getting Started

Before you begin, take a deep breath. This workbook isn't about rushing or performing; it's about noticing, reflecting, and showing up with honesty and grace. Each module focuses on a healing theme and offers two lessons with tools, prompts, and gentle faith reflections. You'll see space to explore your story, respond with curiosity, and take breaks when needed.

Whether you're working through this on your own or in a group, let the pace be kind. If you need to pause, revisit a section, or sit with something longer, that's part of the process. You can write in the book, use a journal, or just reflect as you go.

Also, if you're wondering where to find extra support, turn to the **Appendices** at the back of the book. There, you'll find:

- A simple glossary of terms to help you feel more at ease.

- Index of the tools used throughout the workbook + bonus tools for downloading.

- A short list of books and websites you might find helpful.

- A guide for small groups who want to walk through this together.

- A note for counselors or pastors who may be using the workbook with others.

There's no one right way to move through this material. Start where you are. Pause when you need to.

To my daughter, Korine Martinez,
My granddaughter, Angellee Jones
And all the people who supported me on my journey.

Table of Contents

Module 0: Workbook Introduction 11
Lesson 0.1: Welcome and Workbook Overview............. 11

Lesson 0.2: How to Navigate the Lessons 15

Lesson 0.3: Workbook Objectives..................................... 19

Module 1: The Search for Real Love 23
Lesson 1.1: What I Thought Love Was 23

Lesson 1.2: Beginning to Rewrite the Story 29

Module 2: Silence, Secrets, and Survival 35
Lesson 2.1: Hiding to Feel Safe... 35

Lesson 2.2: When Things Don't Make Sense 42

Module 3: Longing for Safety, Glimpses of Trust 49
Lesson 3.1: Held in the Chaos... 49

Lesson 3.2: Beginning to Trust 55

Module 4: Breaking Point—When Survival Begins to Crack 61
Lesson 4.1: The Pressure to Hold It All Together.......... 61

Lesson 4.2: Cracks That Let the Light In 67

Module 5: Holding It Together–Motherhood, Flashbacks, and the Illusion of Control 73
Lesson 5.1: When Joy and Shame Collide....................... 73

Lesson 5.2: Denial, Distance, and Silent Survival 78

Module 6: When Everything Comes Undone... 83

Lesson 6.1: When the Panic Breaks Through 83

Lesson 6.2: Too Much, Too Fast 89

Module 7: The Edge of Healing 95

Lesson 7.1: When It All Falls Apart 95

Lesson 7.2: Finding Shelter in the Storm 101

Module 8: When Coping Breaks Down 107

Lesson 8.1: When Fear and Grief Blur the Lines 107

Lesson 8.2: Starting Again with Boundaries 112

Module 9: Shame, Self-Worth, and the First Glimpse of Grace 120

Lesson 9.1: The Weight of Shame 120

Lesson 9.2: Love That Doesn't Have to Be Earned ... 126

Module 10: Integration, Grace, and Moving Forward 131

Lesson 10.1: Tools That Help Us Stay Grounded 131

Lesson 10.2: Living What You've Learned 137

Appendices 143

Appendix A: Glossary of Terms 143

Appendix B: Tools and Worksheets Index 146

Appendix C: Additional Resources 150

Appendix D: Small Group Guide 154

Appendix E: A Note for Counselors, Pastors, and Support People 156

Appendix F: About the Author 158

Appendix G: Stay Connected 159

Module 0:

Workbook Introduction

Theme Overview: Starting Gently, Moving with Purpose

Module 0 helps you get your bearings before we delve into deeper healing concepts. Regardless of whether you've read *the memoir*, these introductory lessons will prepare, guide, and support you on your learning journey, promoting wellbeing. You don't have to revisit painful memories to use this workbook effectively. Just start from where you are.

Lesson 0.1:
Welcome and Workbook Overview

Lesson Focus: Setting the Stage for Healing

Welcome to *Faith in the Fog*. I'm so glad you are here. I created this workbook to help you explore your story, reconnect with your sense of worth, and discover how faith and healing can coexist, even when the path feels uncertain. You won't find a list of rules or rigid expectations here. What you will find is compassion, space to reflect, and tools that you can carry forward in your daily life.

This workbook provides a healing journey using trauma-informed and faith-based approaches. Themed lessons, story-based reflections, interactive activities, and gentle spiritual guidance are all included. Whether you learn alone or in a group, this adaptable structure lets you learn at your own pace.

Although prior reading of the memoir isn't necessary, it will enrich the experience for those familiar with it. Each module offers insight and support to help you identify old patterns, reconnect with your inner resilience, and reflect on how God's presence may have been with you, even in the fog.

Is this course/workbook right for you?

Although designed for childhood trauma survivors, this workbook offers valuable insights for:

- Survivors of childhood trauma
- Friends and family of survivors
- Counselors, Therapists, and Social Workers
- Pastors, Lay Ministers, and Small Group leaders
- Teachers, School Counselors

Digging Deeper Activity: Where Am I Starting From?

Before diving into this workbook, take a moment to pause and reflect. Everyone's healing journey is deeply personal and begins at a different point. You might be here for clarity, or maybe a past event has you feeling stuck. This is a judgment-free and expectation-free space for you to explore and grow, no matter your starting point.

Consider the prompts below to think about why you're using this workbook.

Why are you here?

What are you hoping for as you begin this workbook?

How would you define "healing" at this moment?

> ***Note from Charlotte***
>
> It's all right if you're unsure what this offers you. Showing up is already a brave and wonderful first step. Self-honesty: that's all that matters.

Reflection

How does it feel to express your hopes?

_____
_____
_____
_____
_____

What worries you about beginning?

_____
_____
_____
_____
_____

Optional Facebook Group Prompt

What's one word that describes where you're beginning this adventure? You're invited to share it in the Lesson 0.1 thread.

_____
_____
_____
_____
_____

Lesson 0.2:
How to Navigate the Lessons

Lesson Focus: Finding Your Pace and Path

Each module centers on a healing theme and includes:

- A short commentary to introduce the emotional and spiritual focus.

- Two lessons: one reflective, one practical -Each lesson has a summary of the relevant chapters.

- "Digging Deeper" activities that help you apply what you're learning.

- Theme aligned reflections (including optional scriptures)

- Optional Facebook Group prompts for those who want to share in community.

- A theme focused resource box with book, podcast, and website suggestions at the end of each module.

This workbook isn't linear. Some progress steadily, lesson by lesson. Others reread sections or pause often. There's no wrong way to do this.

Where to Get Added Help:

• Download printable tools and optional worksheets here: https://charlottethomason.com/downloads
• Access the private workbook Facebook group directory here:
https://charlottethomason.com/forum

Digging Deeper Activity: How Do I Learn Best?

The processes of learning and healing are often messy, unpredictable, and deeply personal adventures. Before you start, think about the best way for you to work through this workbook. How you learn is equally important to what you learn. This isn't a one-size-fits-all situation; therefore, begin by asking yourself:

Among journaling, drawing, talking, and silent reflection, which do you prefer?

Which of these helps you feel grounded: silence, music, movement, or nature?

> ***Note from Charlotte***
>
> The process of healing is unique to each person. What's successful for others might not work for you. That's all right. Discover your own pace and what provides you with a sense of safety and stability.

Reflection

Can you describe a method for creating a safe space (mentally or physically) while working through this workbook?

_____
_____
_____
_____
_____
_____
_____

Optional Facebook Group Prompt

Which aspect of your learning style are you prioritizing here?

_____
_____
_____
_____
_____
_____
_____
_____

Share your thoughts in the Lesson 0.2 thread.

Lesson 0.3: Workbook Objectives

Lesson Focus: Why This Matters

Faith in the Fog isn't about perfection or accomplishment, it's about discovery. I created each lesson to walk with you, not fix you. They are invitations to reflect, reframe, and reconnect with who you are and how you've survived.

By the end of this course, I hope you will:

- **Feel** less alone in your story

- **Notice** patterns in your emotional and spiritual responses

- **Consider** how past beliefs shaped your view of love, worth, and safety.

- **Learn** simple tools to stay present when hard emotions rise

- **Link** your faith and healing in ways that provide comfort and purpose.

- **Replace** shame with compassion and performance with grace

- **Keep** handy practices you can revisit.

The lessons are not milestones to achieve. They're moments to live with.

Digging Deeper Activity: Setting Intentions

Take a moment to review the objectives listed above.

Reflect: What feels authentic to your current path? Pick some objectives that speak to you and let them guide your reflections.

Workbook Objective	Does this have significance for me?	Notes or thoughts

> **Note from Charlotte**
>
> The objectives aren't checklists to complete. Rather, they are invitations to consider, grow, and rest when needed. You don't have to do everything at once. Just choose a few that feel important at this moment.

Reflection

What are your hopes for your recovery journey in this season?

_____
_____
_____
_____

What would "gentle progress" look like for you?

_____
_____
_____
_____

Optional Facebook Group Prompt

Which workbook objective feels most meaningful to you currently? You're invited to share in the Lesson 0.3 thread.

_____
_____
_____

A Note About Triggers and Support

These lessons in this workbook could trigger strong emotions or memories, which may require you to rest, stop, or ask for help. If this happens, be kind to yourself and take the time you need before continuing the course. Also, if you feel overwhelmed, please connect with a counselor, trusted friend, or support person. Remember, you needn't face healing by yourself.

> Disclaimer: This workbook should not replace professional counseling and you should important to seek professional help If you are struggling with severe depression, anxiety, or suicidal thoughts.

Lesson 0.4: Join the Workbook Facebook Group

I've created optional, private Facebook groups for support with each workbook/course designed to encourage connections with fellow participants.

The complete *group* list is available here:

https://charlottethomason.com/forum

Module 1:

The Search for Real Love

Theme Overview

This module examines how our early experiences influence our perceptions of love, particularly the notion that love must be earned by conforming to certain standards, such as being small, doing the right things, or remaining silent. To begin rewriting that story, you're invited to examine those old beliefs and begin replacing them with truth.

Lesson 1.1:
What I Thought Love Was

Lesson Focus

We often form our earliest definitions of love before we can name them. This lesson helps you discover how your childhood experiences shaped your expectations of love and connection.

Memoir Vignette

In Chapter 1, I invite you into my early childhood, where my understanding of love started taking shape. I explained my understanding of those near me and my concept of love. Those first impressions settled deep, shaping how I would respond to both care and harm as I grew.

Digging Deeper Activity: Create a 'Love Map'

Let's take a moment to reflect on your personal experiences with love. This activity is all about unpacking what love has meant to you, your emotional response to it, and how you've come to understand it over time. There's no right or wrong approach; it's about being honest with yourself and exploring your story.

Here's what you can do: use the space below, grab a piece of paper, a notebook, or even some art supplies if the mood strikes you. Use words, drawings, or even colors to express your thoughts. There are a few prompts to get you started:

Love looked like:

_____
_____
_____
_____
_____
_____
_____
_____
_____
_____
_____
_____

Love sounded like:

Love felt like:

I believed I was loved when:

Take your time with this. This is your space to explore freely and maybe even discover something new about yourself.

> ***Note from Charlotte***
>
> Some of the hardest beliefs to change are the ones we learned before we had the words to question them. For a long time, I didn't even know I was working from a belief that love had to be earned. I just thought that's how the world worked. If that's true for you too, please give yourself grace. You weren't wrong for trying to understand love; you were just learning with the tools you had.

Reflection

What surprised you about your love map?

Which part still affects how you relate to others or God?

Optional Scripture

"See what great love the Father has lavished on us..." **1 John 3:1 (NIV)**

Reflection: What would "lavished" love feel like compared to what you mapped?

Faith in the Fog

Scripture says God has lavished love on us, but that can sound like poetry when we're used to scraps. If 'lavished' feels out of reach, just start here: You are not invisible to God. He sees the version of you that doesn't need to perform. The version that's just... you. And He calls that version His child.

Optional Facebook Group Prompt

What's one word or image from your love map that helped you recognize a pattern you're ready to outgrow? You're invited to share your response in the Lesson 1.1 thread.

Lesson 1.2:
Beginning to Rewrite the Story

Lesson Focus

As we uncover old beliefs, we can begin the slow, grace-filled work of choosing something different. This lesson offers space to name the lies and practice new truths.

Memoir Vignette

In these chapters, silence became part of the air I breathed. I learned some things were better left unspoken, and that confusion was something you just lived with. Chapters 2 and 3 describe a growing awareness that things were not as they should be, yet no one seemed to say so. These chapters reflect how the absence of open conversation can lead to emotional confusion and internalized shame. Even in the middle of the silence and confusion, I held onto the belief that Jesus was listening.

Digging Deeper Activity: Replacing Old Beliefs

Some of our beliefs might have served us well at one time, or they may have provided comfort or protection when life felt overwhelming, but now, they might be holding us back from living in freedom and grace. This activity helps release unhelpful beliefs, replacing them with life-giving truths.

Here's how you can approach it:

Use the space below, grab a piece of paper, a journal, or even open a fresh note on your phone. Start by thinking about the old beliefs that seem to pop up in your mind during challenging moments. Don't worry about making everything perfect; this is just a chance to notice and name them.

- Next, create two columns or use two separate sections, or use the table below. Label one side "Old Belief" and the other "New Truth I Want to Practice."
- In the "Old Belief" column, jot down as many outdated or limiting beliefs as you can without pressuring yourself. This isn't about digging too deep all at once. It's about taking the first step.
- Then, in the "New Truth" column, write a truth that you want to embrace to counter each old belief. Think of truths that remind you of your inherent worth and the unconditional love you're surrounded by.
- Remember, this isn't a race. Replacing old beliefs takes time, patience, and daily acts of courage. Celebrate each small step forward!

Take a breath, approach this with kindness toward yourself, and trust the process. You're doing something brave and beautiful by choosing to rewrite your story, one truth at a time.

Old Belief	New Truth I Want to Practice
Ex. I am loved only when I'm good.	Ex. I am loved because God created me.

> ### *Note from Charlotte*
>
> Sometimes the hardest part of healing is letting go of a belief that once kept us safe. You don't have to rush this. Naming the belief is a big step. Practicing a new truth is a daily act of courage.

Reflection

Which 'New Truth' do you want to practice this week?

_____
_____
_____
_____
_____
_____
_____

What might change if you lived from that truth for one day?

_____
_____
_____
_____
_____
_____
_____
_____

Optional Scripture

"The Lord your God... will rejoice over you with singing."
Zephaniah 3:17 (NIV)

Reflection: What would it feel like to be rejoiced over?

Faith in the Fog

It's difficult to accept God's joy in us when we've dedicated our lives to earning His approval. But what if it's true? What if He's not watching to judge you, but watching with joy because He loves who you are becoming? Even in the fog, His voice is still singing.

Optional Facebook Group Prompt

Which old belief did you choose to reframe? You're invited to share your chart (or just one line from it) in the Lesson 1.2 thread.

Module 1 Resource Box: The Search for Real Love

Want to Go a Little Deeper?

If something stirred in you during this module, you're not alone. Past experiences of love (or the lack of it) shape so much of how we see ourselves and God. If you're curious to explore more, here are a few gentle resources that may offer encouragement and insight.

Book: *The Soul of Shame* by **Curt Thompson**
A thoughtful, faith-based exploration of how shame distorts our view of ourselves—and how God's love invites us toward healing and connection.

Podcast: *The Next Right Thing* by **Emily P. Freeman**

(Episode 1: "Become a Soul Minimalist") These short, reflective episodes offer quiet clarity and spiritual grounding for those in transition or healing.

Website: The Attachment Project
www.attachmentproject.com This site offers simple, research-based tools to help you understand how past relationships influence your patterns of connection

Module 2:

Silence, Secrets, and Survival

Theme Overview

In this module, we continue exploring the emotional strategies children use to survive what they can't explain: silence, secrecy, withdrawal, and denial. When no one names what's happening, we learn to stay quiet, too. These lessons encourage noticing how those patterns shaped your story and exploring what it means to be seen without shame. Survival didn't equal failure. That's what kept us together.

Lesson 2.1:
Hiding to Feel Safe

Lesson Focus

Sometimes survival means learning to stay small, quiet, and unnoticed, especially when a connection seems unsafe or unpredictable and disappearing seems like the best choice. This lesson encourages you to consider how loneliness, betrayal, or early friendships shaped your view of trust and what it meant to be seen.

Memoir Vignette

In Chapter 4, I share a story from third grade that marked a turning point in how I understood friendship and belonging. I thought I had finally made a friend, someone who gave me a glimpse of what I thought was normal life. However, when she convinced me to do her homework and blamed me when we got caught, it left a deep emotional scar. From this experience, I learned that trusting others could backfire and that it might be safer to stay invisible. Even in that season of loneliness, I found comfort in conversations with Jesus, often retreating to a quiet place in the backyard where I could talk to Him. That small shelter gave me a sense of safety and sometimes I wished I could stay there with Him instead of returning to the confusing world around me.

Digging Deeper Activity: Safe or Small?

In this activity, we're going to explore the moments when we chose invisibility over being seen, and why.

Begin by recalling situations where you thought staying small or invisible was your best choice. What were you protecting yourself from? Once you've recognized those moments, study what you needed at the time, comfort, safety, connection, and consider how those needs might be different today. Use the table below as a guide to organize your thoughts and see how far you've come.

Here's your framework:

When I stayed small: Recall specific instances where you believed shrinking away was your only choice.

Consider what would have provided you with a sense of safety and support.

What I need now: Recognize what you value now and what helps you thrive in your relationships and personal life.

Take your time with this. It's not about judgment; it's about understanding yourself a little better. Growth often starts with noticing the patterns that shaped us.

Let's dive in!

When I stayed small	What I needed then	What I need now

When I stayed small	What I needed then	What I need now

> ### *Note from Charlotte*
>
> Sometimes, smallness becomes a habit, one we don't even recognize until we're older but I was unaware I was choosing invisibility. I just knew that being seen often came with pain or pressure. To find relief, I escaped to the quiet backyard spot that offered more than refuge. It was holy ground where, even when the world appeared unsafe, I remembered Jesus was aware of me and loved me.

Reflection Prompts

What did staying small/invisible protect you from?

_____
_____
_____
_____

Do any of those patterns still show up in your relationships today?

_____
_____
_____
_____

Optional Scripture

"You are my hiding place; you will protect me from trouble and surround me with songs of deliverance." **Psalm 32:7 (NIV)**

Reflection: What is your response to the idea that God is your hiding place?

How do you see Him protecting you from trouble and surrounding you with songs of deliverance?

Faith in the Fog

Sometimes God meets us in the hidden places, not to keep us hidden, but to remind us that we're not alone. Even when no one else understood, He was there, and He still is.

Optional Facebook Group Prompt

What's one way you learned to "stay small" that you're starting to notice and name? You're invited to share your chart (or a single line) in the Lesson 2.1 thread.

Lesson 2.2:
When Things Don't Make Sense

Lesson Focus

Sometimes, the world around us doesn't match what we feel inside. When no one explains what's happening or when things feel too strange to name, we may doubt our instincts or shut down emotionally. This lesson invites you to reflect on moments of confusion and spiritual comfort, and how both can shape our understanding of reality and God.

Memoir Vignette

In Chapter 5, I describe a growing tension in our home. I didn't have the words for what was wrong, but I knew something didn't feel right. I learned not to ask questions. Then in Chapter 6, after a serious incident, I had an experience I couldn't explain; I saw Jesus. That moment was both comforting and confusing. I didn't fully understand what had happened, but I held onto that glimpse of Him because it felt more real than anything else. It was one of the first times I realized maybe God saw me as more than the abuse I experienced.

Digging Deeper Activity: Sorting the Unspoken

Take a few moments to think back on experiences where what you felt inside didn't match what others were saying or doing. It might be a situation where you felt uneasy, but everyone around you acted as if everything was fine, or maybe a time when your instincts told you something was off, but you were told you were overreacting.

Now, use the chart below to explore those moments in more depth. In the first column, jot down what you felt or sensed in that situation, your gut reaction, emotions, or even physical sensations. In the second column, write what others were saying or doing that didn't align with your feelings. Finally, in the third column, reflect on what you needed in that moment but maybe didn't receive.

If nothing comes to you right away, that's okay too. Sometimes, just opening yourself up to the process can be enough for something to surface later. Don't push yourself to recall events.

What I felt or sensed	What others said or did	What I needed

What I felt or sensed	What others said or did	What I needed

> **Note from Charlotte**
>
> Learning to trust yourself again is one of the hardest parts of healing, especially if others taught you to doubt your feelings. I spent years trying to reconcile what I knew inside with what no one else would say aloud. That moment with Jesus didn't erase the confusion, but it gave me an anchor. You don't have to understand everything to begin healing.

Reflection Prompts

What's one moment from your childhood that felt confusing or unexplainable?

_____

What helped you feel safe in the middle of it?

_____

As an adult, how can you help your younger self feel safe in a similar way?

Optional Scripture

Isaiah 41:10 *"So do not fear, for I am with you... I will strengthen you and help you; I will uphold you with my righteous right hand.* **Isaiah 41:10 (NIV)**

Reflection: How would embracing these words affect your belief about yourself and your relationship with God and others?

Faith in the Fog

When everything feels unclear, God doesn't need you to have the right words. He sees what others missed. He holds what didn't make sense and He's not waiting for you to figure it all out before He shows up.

Optional Facebook Group Prompt

What's one way you've started reconnecting with your sense of what's true? You're invited to share your response in the Lesson 2.2 thread.

Module 2 Resource Box: Silence, Secrets, and Survival

Want to Go a Little Deeper?

Survival strategies like silence and secrecy often begin before we even realize we're using them. If this module helped you name patterns that once protected you, but no longer serve you, you're already doing brave work. These resources offer gentle insight into how those patterns form and how they begin to change.

Book: *Try Softer* by **Aundi Kolber**

Written by a licensed therapist who integrates trauma-informed care with Christian faith, this book invites you to stop white-knuckling through life and instead learn to listen to what your body and soul truly need.

Podcast: *The Place We Find Ourselves* with **Adam Young**

This podcast explores how childhood trauma, attachment, and unspoken pain shape our adult lives. Start with episodes on story work, dissociation, or why silence often feels safer.

Website: Allender Center
www.theallendercenter.org A hub for trauma recovery and narrative work, the Allender Center offers articles, podcasts, and courses for those exploring the stories that shaped them.

Module 3:

Longing for Safety, Glimpses of Trust

Theme Overview

In this module, we explore how trust can form even in the middle of fear and chaos. When a child experiences comfort or protection, whether through a safe adult or a spiritual encounter, it leaves a mark. These early moments of hope don't erase the pain, but they offer glimpses of something more: a longing to be known, loved, and safe. This module invites you to revisit those moments where connection, safety, or comfort replaced fear.

Lesson 3.1:
Held in the Chaos

Lesson Focus

Moments of fear and trauma sometimes hold surprising clarity. This lesson explores how divine comfort, or presence can show up even when everything else appears unsafe and how those moments can anchor us later in life.

Memoir Vignette

In Chapter 7, I share a moment when fear overcame me. Something unexplainable took place; however, during the confusion, I sensed Jesus beside me. His presence brought calm, and it stayed with me. I didn't fully grasp it then, but it was one of the few times I experienced an unconditional love not dependent on my behavior or words. It was just there.

Digging Deeper Activity: Anchors in the Storm

This activity allows you to reflect on those small yet powerful moments when comfort, safety, or connection broke through during times of chaos. These memories, though they may seem fleeting or insignificant at first, often carry deep meaning and can provide a sense of grounding even in today's storms. This is a space to explore and honor what those moments mean to you.

Here's what you can do:

Recall a particular memory where you experienced calmness, safety, or a sense of being understood during a frightening moment. It could be something big, like someone comforting you during a crisis, or something small, like hearing a kind word or noticing a peaceful presence.

Use the space below to describe or draw the moment in detail.

As you're reflecting, consider these prompts to guide you:

Faith In The Fog

Where were you? What was happening around you?

_____

How did you feel physically? Were you tense, relaxed, or something else entirely?

_____

What set this moment apart from all the others?

_____
_____
_____
_____
_____
_____
_____
_____
_____
_____
_____

Do you still keep the memory with you today? If so, how does it continue to affect you physically, emotionally, or spiritually?

_____
_____
_____
_____
_____
_____
_____
_____
_____
_____
_____

Feel free to explore these questions in a way which suits you. Reworded 1: Let the moment's message reach you—through words, art, or quiet thought.

> **Note from Charlotte**
>
> I couldn't find the words to explain what occurred then but I, for a few minutes, experienced love and care. Sometimes, the moments we remember most clearly aren't the ones people expect us to. They're the ones that helped us survive.

Reflection Prompts

What's one memory you go back to when everything is hard to handle?

What message about your needs or self-worth do you believe your memory is conveying?

Optional Scripture

"God is our refuge and strength, an ever-present help in trouble."
Psalm 46:1 (NIV)

Reflection: In what way does viewing God as our refuge and strength affect you?

Faith in the Fog

When chaos surrounds us, it's difficult to think God is present, but sometimes His presence isn't loud; it's a quiet presence. If you've ever had such an experience, even for a second, it matters more than you know.

Optional Facebook Group Prompt

What single word or image is your reminder, you're not alone in the chaos? You're invited to share your response in the Lesson 3.1 thread.

Lesson 3.2: Beginning to Trust

Lesson Focus

This lesson explores how we test the waters of trust. Despite betrayal or pain, the heart knows what compassion is. We'll consider those beginning steps to believing that safety and love may be possible.

Memoir Vignette

In Chapter 8, I describe meeting an adult, George, who treated me with gentleness. I was unsure if I could depend on it, but a part of me longed to. I watched carefully, trying to decide if it was true. Those early interactions planted a seed of hope, but his compassion confused me. He wanted nothing from me, and I could not understand his actions.

Digging Deeper Activity: Trust Checkpoints

Think back to a time when someone extended kindness toward you, and you found yourself unsure how to react. Maybe it was a slight gesture, such as a person holding the door for you, or something bigger, such as an offer of help when you needed it.

Spend a moment to reflect:

What made you hesitate? Was it fear, doubt, or perhaps a sense of unfamiliarity?

What did you wish to believe in that instance? Were you hoping for compassion to be genuine?

Now consider today:

What could help you feel safe enough to trust someone's kindness?

_____
_____
_____
_____
_____
_____
_____
_____
_____

Could it be time, consistency, or perhaps allowing yourself to take a slight chance?

_____
_____
_____
_____
_____
_____
_____
_____
_____

Jot down your thoughts above and, if you feel comfortable, share them with a trusted friend or write them in your journal. Think of this as a gentle way to explore your relationship with trust and the hope that kindness can be real and meaningful.

> ### *Note from Charlotte*
>
> If someone hurts you, even kindness can seem suspicious. I did not know how to react at the beginning, but deep down, I hoped it was real. That desire for love is a source of strength, not weakness.

Reflection Prompts

How have you experienced hope, despite not being sure you could rely on it?

_____
_____
_____
_____
_____
_____
_____
_____

How do you react when someone offers you kindness now?

_____
_____
_____
_____
_____
_____
_____
_____

Optional Scripture

"May the God of hope fill you with all joy and peace as you trust in him…" **Romans 15:13 (NIV)**

Reflection: What would it mean for you to be filled with joy and peace?

Faith in the Fog

Disappointment might make hope seem dangerous, but it's also holy and your hesitation does not intimidate God. He meets you in the pause, the questions, the longing and He stays.

Optional Facebook Group Prompt

What's one thing that gives you hope, even if you're still learning how to trust? You're invited to share your response in the Lesson 3.2 thread.

Module 3 Resource Box: Longing for Safety, Glimpses of Trust

Want to Go a Little Deeper?

Even in the middle of fear, our hearts remember what it's like to feel safe, if only for a moment. This module invites us to honor the glimpses of hope and connection we may have experienced along the way. These resources offer encouragement for rebuilding trust and noticing the small ways God and others show up.

Book: Safe People by Dr. Henry Cloud & **Dr. John Townsend**

A helpful guide to recognizing the kinds of relationships that nurture healing—and those that don't. Especially helpful if trust feels risky or confusing.

Podcast: *Unspoken: Stories of Trauma and Healing*

This storytelling podcast features first-person accounts of trauma recovery, often highlighting the quiet moments that led to breakthrough. Look for episodes on connection and trust.

Website: *Grace Alliance* - **Mental Health Resources**
www.mentalhealthgracealliance.org
This faith-based organization provides free guides, devotional tools, and support materials for those navigating emotional health and trauma.

Module 4:

Breaking Point—When Survival Begins to Crack

Theme Overview

Sometimes we don't realize how hard we've been trying until everything falls apart. When old coping strategies stop working, the feelings we've kept buried start breaking through. In this module, we look at the quiet unraveling that can happen even when we're still performing well on the outside. This isn't failure, it's what happens when your heart is finally too full to carry the silence alone. These lessons encourage you to approach this space with honesty, allowing you to name and reflect on your burdens without judgment or shame.

Lesson 4.1:
The Pressure to Hold It All Together

Lesson Focus

Sometimes, we get so good at bottling up pain and putting on a brave face but we forget to notice what's really falling apart inside.

This lesson explores what it costs to keep holding everything in, and what it means to notice the cracks without judging or shaming ourselves.

Memoir Vignette

In Chapter 10, I share how I started to feel like something was deeply wrong inside me, even though I couldn't explain it.

I was still going to school, still doing what I was supposed to do, but I felt like I was falling apart. No one knew. I didn't even know what to call it, but I remember moments of panic and sadness that made little sense, like I was breaking from the inside.

Digging Deeper Activity: What Holding It Together Looks Like

Before jumping into these questions, take a breather and give yourself a little time to think. The goal is to explore what is going on beneath the surface and acknowledge it.

Journaling exercise:

What's the story I present to others?

What's happening underneath that story?

What does my body feel like when I'm doing this?

What are some things you do to calm down when you are anxious?

Which of your coping strategies are healthy, and which may be destructive?

> ### *Note from Charlotte*
>
> I didn't know I was falling apart; I just knew I couldn't breathe. I was doing everything "right," but something inside me was coming loose. Looking back, I can see that the unraveling wasn't a weakness. It was the beginning of honesty.

Optional Scripture

"My grace is sufficient for you, for my power is made perfect in weakness…" **2 Corinthians 12:9 (NIV)**

Reflection: What if your unraveling isn't the end but the beginning of God meeting you in a deeper way?

_____
_____
_____
_____
_____
_____
_____
_____
_____
_____

> ### *Faith in the Fog*
>
> When you've spent a lifetime managing pain in silence, it can feel terrifying to admit you're not okay, but God doesn't ask us to hold everything alone. Sometimes the most sacred thing we can do is whisper, 'I can't do this by myself.' That whisper is a prayer and He hears it.

Reflection Prompt

What part of your story have you kept hidden because it felt like it was too much?

_____
_____
_____
_____
_____
_____
_____
_____
_____
_____

What would it look like to let someone see that part, even just a little?

_____
_____
_____
_____
_____
_____
_____
_____
_____

Optional Facebook Group Prompt

What's one word that describes how it feels to keep it all together and what might change if you didn't have to? Please share your response in the Lesson 4.1 thread.

Lesson 4.2: Cracks That Let the Light In

Lesson Focus

Even in the middle of unraveling, we sometimes experience unexpected grace through a conversation, a memory, a moment of stillness that reminds us of we're not completely alone. This lesson is about recognizing those glimmers, not as fixes, but as reminders that hope can survive the dark.

Memoir Vignette

In Chapter 11, a childhood pastor unexpectedly visited me and gave me communion.

He didn't know I was spiraling or that I'd considered ending my life. That minor act of grace, reminding me that others still saw me, helped me choose to stay. That communion moment stayed with me, like a soft thread of hope I didn't fully understand yet.

In Chapter 12, I got married, believing it might fix the broken parts. But the shame didn't disappear.

> **Note from Charlotte**
>
> One of the hardest things to accept was that grace didn't always come in big, obvious ways. It often came through people who showed up at the right time, or a quiet moment when I felt less alone. I didn't recognize it as grace at the time, but now I do.

Digging Deeper Activity: Grace Moments List

Spend some time reflecting on your experiences. Then, jot down 1–3 moments where you felt a sense of relief, connection, or even just the smallest flicker of hope. These don't have to be grand or dramatic; sometimes they're as simple as a kind word, a smile, or a quiet moment that surprised you.

Now, think about:

What made those moments stand out to you?

_____
_____
_____
_____
_____
_____
_____
_____

How did those moments change how you viewed yourself or your worth, even just a little?

Optional Scripture

"A bruised reed he will not break, and a smoldering wick he will not snuff out." **Isaiah 42:3– (NIV)**

Reflection: Where have you felt like a bruised reed or a smoldering wick and what does it mean that God chooses not to break or snuff you out?

> ### *Faith in the Fog*
>
> In college, I started having strange body memories, panic, nausea, confusion, without knowing why. I thought nothing "bad" had happened to me, but my body told a different story. I didn't recognize it as trauma. I just thought I was broken. What I didn't realize then was that even in that confusion, God hadn't left. He was already at work, gently letting the truth rise to the surface.

Reflection Prompt

What's one moment that felt like a flicker of hope, even if you didn't recognize it at the time?

How do you respond to small moments of grace? Do you notice them, doubt them, push them away, or lean in?

Optional Facebook Group Prompt

What's one grace moment you've experienced, something small but meaningful, that reminded you that hope is still possible? You're invited to share your response in the Lesson 4.2 thread.

Module 4 Resource Box: Breaking Point—When Survival Begins to Crack

Want to Go a Little Deeper?

Sometimes the unraveling is what finally brings honesty. If you've reached a point where holding it all together isn't working anymore, you're not failing, you're beginning. These resources offer gentle reflections on what it means to fall apart without shame and begin healing with grace.

Book: *Permission to Feel* by Marc Brackett Written by a leading researcher in emotional intelligence, this book helps readers understand and name their emotions. It's not faith-based, but it offers practical tools that can support healing from emotional overload.

Podcast: *The Best of You* with **Dr. Alison Cook**

(Episode: "What If Falling Apart Is Part of Healing?") This episode explores how breakdowns can signal the beginning of emotional and spiritual growth. Dr. Cook blends psychology and faith in a compassionate, relatable way.

Website: Brené Brown's Atlas of the Heart
www.brenebrown.com/atlas. This visual glossary of emotions helps name what many survivors struggle to describe. Helpful for those learning to name and express inner experiences.

Module 5:

Holding It Together– Motherhood, Flashbacks, and the Illusion of Control

Theme Overview

This module explores how we try to keep going when everything inside us feels like it's breaking. For many survivors, early adulthood is full of pressure to "be okay," especially when others are counting on us. These chapters reflect the tension between loving others deeply and feeling disconnected from yourself. In this module, you're invited to reflect on the masks you wore, the memories that surfaced, and the ways you tried to survive without falling apart.

Lesson 5.1:
When Joy and Shame Collide

Lesson Focus

Life's most beautiful moments are sometimes interwoven with grief, shame, and confusion. This lesson invites you to explore how it feels when something good (like becoming a parent) lives side by side with unhealed pain and self-doubt.

Memoir Vignette

In Chapter 13, I share about the birth of my daughter, a moment filled with both awe and overwhelming shame. I loved her fiercely, but I felt unworthy of being her mother. At the same time, my body remembered things I couldn't explain. The flashbacks were confusing, and I didn't know what they meant. I thought I was losing my mind. Still, in the middle of that pain, there were glimmers of love I couldn't deny.

Digging Deeper Activity: Holding Two Truths

Before diving into the journal prompts below, take a moment to settle into a quiet space where you feel comfortable reflecting. Let yourself be honest and vulnerable; there are no right or wrong answers, just your truth. It's okay if this brings up mixed emotions; allow yourself to sit with them gently. You might want to jot down your thoughts, draw, or simply think about them as you go.

Use the journal prompts below to reflect on moments when you felt both joy and pain:

Describe a time when you experienced something beautiful while also struggling emotionally.

_____
_____
_____
_____
_____
_____
_____

What message did you internalize during that time about your worth?

What would you say now to the version of yourself who was carrying both joy and shame?

> ### *Note from Charlotte*
>
> It's okay if something that was supposed to be joyful also holds sadness. You're not broken for feeling both. You're human and the fact that you kept going, even with all those conflicting emotions, says so much about your strength.

Optional Scripture

"The Lord is close to the brokenhearted and saves those who are crushed in spirit." **Psalm 34:18 (NIV)**

Reflection: What does it mean that God is near? Even when you feel crushed by emotions that you can't name.

_____

_____

_____

_____

_____

_____

_____

_____

_____

> ### *Faith in the Fog*
>
> When I felt ashamed, I thought God could love my daughter but couldn't possibly love me, but now I realize He didn't divide His love; even when I couldn't feel it. If you're doubting God's presence in your pain, remember, love doesn't always feel loud. Sometimes it's just the grace to help us hold on.

Reflection Prompt

When have you felt torn between joy and pain?

What permission do you need to give yourself to feel both without guilt?

Optional Facebook Group Prompt

What's one message you would share with someone who is trying to hold it all together right now? Or, if that's you, what would you tell yourself? You're invited to share your response in the Lesson 5.1 thread.

Lesson 5.2:
Denial, Distance, and Silent Survival

Lesson Focus

Sometimes we survive by stepping back emotionally and disconnecting from what's too heavy to feel. This lesson invites you to notice how silence, denial, or distance may have once helped you cope and how they might still shape your present.

Memoir Vignette

In Chapter 14, I withdrew emotionally even as I tried to be a good mother. I buried my feelings and pretended everything was fine. It felt safer to avoid hard truths than to face what might be underneath. Even when I noticed signs that something was wrong, I kept going. My daughter's childlike faith comforted me, but I couldn't yet grasp that it could apply to me, too.

Digging Deeper Activity: What Silence Protected

Silence, denial, or emotional distance might have been your way of coping, and that's okay. Before answering the questions, think about the situations where you used these strategies, whether it was to protect yourself or simply survive.

Now, make a list of the roles that silence, denial, or emotional distance played in your life:

Question	
When did staying silent feel safer than speaking?	
What emotions or memories might that silence have been protecting you from?	
Reflect on aspects of yourself or your experiences that have yet to find expression.	

Note from Charlotte

I thought being quiet made me strong. I didn't realize that silence can also become a prison. You may not be ready to break that silence all at once and that's okay. Even acknowledging it is a powerful step forward.

Optional Scripture
Psalm 56:8 (NLT)

"You keep track of all my sorrows.
You have collected all my tears in your bottle.
You have recorded each one in your book."

Reflection: What does it mean to you that God notices even the tears you never cried aloud?

Faith in the Fog

God didn't need me to speak perfectly to Him before He could hear me. He was already listening. Even the words I couldn't form, even the prayers I never said aloud, He heard them. If you've been silent for a long time, know this: you are not forgotten.

Reflection Prompt
What does silence continue to protect you from?

Faith In The Fog

What would it mean to give voice to what's been unspoken?

Optional Facebook Group Prompt

Is there a moment where you chose silence that now feels ready to be spoken or at least acknowledged? You're invited to share your response in the Lesson 5.2 thread.

Module 5 Resource Box: Holding It Together – Motherhood, Flashbacks, and the Illusion of Control

Want to Go a Little Deeper?

This module touches the tender space where love and shame often collide. If you've tried to hold everything together while silently unraveling inside, you're not alone. These resources gently explore the tension between caring for others and staying connected to yourself.

Book: *Mother Hunger* by **Kelly McDaniel**

Written especially for women whose early attachment wounds affect their adult relationships, this book explores the ache for nurturing that many carry. It's insightful for mothers—and for daughters still healing.

Podcast: *Grace for the Journey*

(Episode: "When You're Doing Too Much") A short, soulful conversation on burnout, emotional overload, and learning to pause with compassion. Encouraging for anyone trying to balance caregiving and healing.

Website: *Postpartum Support International* (for more than postpartum) www.postpartum.net. Though originally designed for new parents, this site includes resources for anyone managing emotional distress while parenting, including trauma survivors navigating flashbacks and fatigue.

Module 6:

When Everything Comes Undone

Theme Overview

This module reflects the moment when the pain you've been carrying surfaces and it's too much to manage on your own anymore. It's where healing moves from theory to reality, but that shift can feel like collapse before it feels like growth. Here, we explore what it means to unravel emotionally while still holding onto faith and how grounding tools and grace can help us stay present through the storm.

Lesson 6.1:
When the Panic Breaks Through

Lesson Focus

This lesson explores what happens when a current experience triggers past trauma and you don't yet have the words to name what's happening. It's about facing memories you didn't know you had, and how moments of spiritual clarity can still appear in chaos.

Memoir Vignette

In Chapter 15, my daughter's baptism should have been a moment of joy. Instead, it triggered panic, confusion, and flashbacks I didn't understand. In the middle of that emotional chaos, I saw Jesus showing me a thorn-covered path. He pointed to women tangled in the bushes and told me, "You can't help them until you heal." At that moment, something broke open in me. I knew I needed help, but I didn't yet know how deep the pain would go.

Digging Deeper Activity: Grounding When Triggered

When overwhelming emotions or body memories take over, it can feel like you're spinning out of control, disconnected from the present moment, or even from yourself. This grounding tool is important because it helps you break that cycle, reconnect with your surroundings, and reminds you that you are safe. It's a simple yet powerful way to regain a sense of stability and take care of yourself during difficult moments.

Soothing Object Exercise

Step 1: Pick an object that feels comforting to you—a stone, a keychain, a cross, or any item you can carry with you. Keep it somewhere accessible, like in your pocket, your bag, or even next to your bed.

Step 2: When you feel triggered or overwhelmed, grab the object and hold it in your hand. Take a moment to notice how it feels—its texture, temperature, or weight.

Step 3: Ask yourself these questions:

How old do I feel right now? Is this feeling from the present or the past?

Where am I right now? Look around and remind yourself of your surroundings.

What do I see that shows me I'm safe? Perhaps a locked door, a loved one nearby, or familiar surroundings comfort you.

Step 4: Think about what you need at this moment. Try deep breaths, prayer, or stillness.

Bonus Tip: Don't rush through the steps! Let the process unfold at your own pace. Jot down your reflections afterward if it helps but remember, there's no "right" way to do this. You're simply giving yourself a chance to connect and stay grounded.

Jot a few notes afterward: How did that moment pass? What helped you stay present?

> ### *Note from Charlotte*
>
> I didn't know what was happening. I just knew something was wrong. The vision helped me recognize that healing couldn't wait anymore. But that didn't mean I was ready to go fast. If you're here, facing unexpected emotions, let yourself take it slow. Awareness is enough for today.

Optional Scripture

"So do not fear, for I am with you... I will strengthen you and help you..." **Isaiah 41:10 (NIV)**

Reflection: What if God's presence is strongest when your grip is weakest?

_____
_____
_____
_____
_____
_____
_____
_____
_____
_____

> ### *Faith in the Fog*
>
> That vision felt like a gift and a challenge. It showed me I wasn't alone, but it also asked me to change. I've learned that when God asks us to heal, He also stays with us through every messy step. You don't have to figure everything out to be held by Him.

Reflection Prompt

What recent moment brought up emotions you didn't expect?

What helped or could help you stay present at that moment?

If you used the "Soothing Object Exercise," describe the experience.

Optional Facebook Group Prompt

Has a recent experience caught you off guard emotionally? What small actions helped you feel safe again, or what might help next time? You're invited to share your response in the Lesson 6.1 thread.

Lesson 6.2:
Too Much, Too Fast

Lesson Focus

This lesson explores what happens when we push too hard to heal and end up overwhelmed. It's about recognizing your limits, honoring your pace, and choosing compassion over urgency.

Memoir Vignette

In Chapter 16, I began therapy and charged into healing with everything I had. I returned to the places where my childhood pain lived, hoping that confronting it would bring freedom. Instead, I became overwhelmed. The memories came faster than I could process them. I withdrew emotionally, pushed people away, and started to fall apart. The truth is, I didn't know how to go slow. I thought healing had to be fast, and I almost broke under that pressure.

Digging Deeper Activity: My Healing Pace

Sometimes, life gets so busy, or emotions feel so overwhelming, that we forget to slow down and listen to ourselves. That's okay, it happens to all of us. What's important is finding little pockets of time to check in with your heart, your mind, and your body. Healing isn't about rushing to the finish line; it's about showing up with kindness and patience for yourself.

To help you do just that, here's a journal prompt to guide you through these reflections. Be honest but also remember to treat yourself with compassion and not push too hard. You're just about creating space for your thoughts, no matter where you're at in the process.

Take your time, breathe, and see where these questions lead you:

Right now, my healing feels…

Think about how your healing process feels at this moment. Are you feeling rushed, stuck, peaceful, or overwhelmed? Write your thoughts honestly because there's no right or wrong answer here.

I notice these signs when I'm going too fast

Pay attention to the signals your mind and body give you. Are you more tired than usual? Feeling irritable or anxious? Maybe you find yourself zoning out or feeling disconnected. Jot down the signs that pop up when you're pushing yourself too hard.

One gentle change I can make this week is…

___

This is where you can take small, intentional steps toward balance. Maybe it's about taking a break from heavy emotional work, limiting how much you try to process at once, or reaching out to someone you trust for support. Be specific about what you can try; it's all about making healing feel just a little lighter.

Remember, healing isn't a race, and there's no finish line waiting for you to cross. It's about showing up for yourself in a way that feels kind and sustainable. You've got this!

> ### *Note from Charlotte*
>
> I thought I could get it all done, tear off the bandage and be free. But healing doesn't work that way. It's not a checklist or a sprint. It's a relationship, with yourself, your story, and with God. And relationships take time. Please, don't push yourself to collapse like I did. You deserve a gentler way.

Optional Scripture

"Come to me, all you who are weary and burdened, and I will give you rest." **Matthew 11:28 (NIV)**

Reflection: What would it look like to approach healing as rest, not as work?

_____
_____
_____
_____
_____
_____
_____
_____
_____

> ### *Faith in the Fog*
>
> God wasn't in a hurry with me. He didn't rush me. He stayed. When I fell apart, He didn't turn away. He simply waited until I could breathe again. If you're running out of steam, rest in that truth: you don't have to earn His presence.

Reflection Prompt

What signs tell you that you're going too fast?

What would it mean to choose rest as part of your healing?

Optional Facebook Group Prompt

What's one thing you've done to slow down your healing process when it felt overwhelming? Share your tips in the Lesson 6.2 thread. Your experience might help someone else.

Module 6 Resource Box: When Everything Comes Undone

Want to Go a Little Deeper?

When the pain surfaces faster than you can process it, it can feel like you're falling apart—but that's often the moment healing becomes real. If this module stirred intense memories or emotions, these resources offer grounding, validation, and tools for moving gently through the fog.

Book: *The Body Keeps the Score* by **Bessel van der Kolk** A foundational book on how trauma lives in the body—and how we can reconnect with ourselves. It's dense, but many survivors find it helpful when they're ready to understand what's happening beneath the surface.

Podcast: *The Mindful Kind* (**Episode:** *"How to Cope with Emotional Overwhelm"*) Short, calming episodes that teach practical strategies for slowing down and staying grounded. Especially helpful when emotions feel too big.

Website: *Trauma Healing Basics* – **National Institute for the Clinical Application of Behavioral Medicine** www.nicabm.com/trauma Offers free videos and articles that explain trauma responses in gentle, accessible language—useful for both survivors and support people.

Module 7:

The Edge of Healing

Theme Overview

There comes a point in every healing journey when the old ways of coping stop working, but the new ways haven't fully formed yet. This in-between space can feel like collapse, but it's also where something true begins. In this module, you're invited to notice what starts to shift when you stop pretending everything's fine. These lessons offer gentle support for the moments when things fall apart, and they hold space for grace, self-care, and the slow rebuild that follows.

Lesson 7.1:
When It All Falls Apart

Lesson Focus

This lesson explores the moment when everything you've relied on breaks down. Sometimes we need things to fall apart so we can stop pretending we're okay and begin the actual work of healing.

Memoir Vignette

In Chapter 17, I reached my limit. I left my job, divorced my husband, and let go of everything I had been trying to hold together. On the surface, it could have looked like a failure. But inside, I knew I couldn't keep surviving on sheer willpower. It was terrifying, but it was also the beginning of something honest.

Digging Deeper Activity: Naming the Ruins

Sometimes, life throws us into moments where everything seems to fall apart, and the pieces we've been holding onto scatter beyond our grasp. It can feel heavy, confusing, even terrifying, but it can also be the start of something honest and new. This activity is here to help you gently make sense of the things that have come undone and consider what might bloom from the space they leave behind.

Here's how you can begin: Let the questions below guide your reflection.

What am I no longer able to carry (emotionally, spiritually, physically)?

_____
_____
_____
_____
_____
_____
_____
_____
_____

Think about the burdens you've been holding, whether it's expectations, roles, or fears—and let yourself name them.

What losses am I grieving, even if I chose them?

Sometimes, the decisions we make for our good could bring sadness. What are you letting go of, and how does it feel?

What do I hope might grow from this place of surrender?

In the clearing where the old ways crumble, what possibilities appear? What small hopes can you nurture here?

Remember, what feels like breaking may simply be the ground shifting to make space for something new. You don't have to fix anything right now, just notice the ground beneath you and trust that healing will follow in its own time.

Note from Charlotte

This was when I stopped trying to be strong. I couldn't fake it anymore. I thought I had lost everything, but what I had really lost was the illusion of control. That loss hurt deeply, but it also made room for real healing to begin.

Optional Scripture

"My grace is sufficient for you, for my power is made perfect in weakness…" **2 Corinthians 12:9(NIV)**

Reflection: What if your breaking point is where God's strength can meet you most tenderly?

Faith in the Fog

God didn't come to me with a blueprint or a rescue plan. He came as a presence, quiet and constant. I didn't need to hold it all together anymore and neither do you.

Reflection Prompt

What illusions or roles are you beginning to let go of?

When might surrender be a sign of strength?

Optional Facebook Group Prompt

If you've reached a breaking point, what has helped you begin again, or what might help you now? Share your response in the Lesson 7.1 thread.

Lesson 7.2:
Finding Shelter in the Storm

Lesson Focus

This lesson is about beginning again with deep care. It explores what it means to let others help you hold the pieces, and how moments of safety can start to rebuild what trauma tried to steal.

Memoir Vignette

In Chapter 18, I entered a six-week inpatient program where the intensity of my emotions almost overwhelmed me, but for the first time, I was in a place that felt safe. Afterward, I joined an intensive outpatient program at a psychiatric hospital. I couldn't work, and I was emotionally raw, but something important shifted. My younger self felt seen. I wasn't being asked to perform; I was just allowed to be and that simple care started the long, slow rebuild toward wholeness.

Digging Deeper Activity: My Self-Care in Crisis–Worksheet

Here's a step-by-step checklist to help you create a plan for those overwhelming moments. This isn't just about having tools, it's about giving yourself the care and stability you deserve when everything feels like too much. Think of it as a safety net you can rely on, one you design for yourself, because no one knows what you need better than you do.

- Recognize the signs: What tells you that you're feeling emotionally overwhelmed? (Examples:

racing thoughts, numbness, flashbacks, fatigue, or feeling frozen.)

Write down what you notice in yourself when things begin to feel too much.

- **Find your grounding tools:** These are practical things you can do to feel more present and steadier.

  - Maybe it's holding something soothing, like a soft blanket or a familiar object. (Soothing Object Tool in Lesson 6.1)

  - Could a quiet prayer or deep breathing exercises help?

  - Gentle movement, like stretching or walking, might work too.

  - Listening to calming music is another choice that may work.

Jot down what has worked for you in the past or what you'd like to try.

- **Define your safe spaces: Name places or memories that help you feel calm and secure.** (A physical location where you feel at ease, a comforting memory or mental image that makes you feel safe, someone you trust and can reach out to for support)

- **Hold on to truth and encouragement: When things feel heavy, what words or ideas lift you?** A scripture verse, mantra, or phrase that reminds you that you're not alone: This could be anything meaningful to you, something that makes you feel understood and anchored.

Permit yourself to pause: Sometimes, the best thing you can do is take a break. Step away from what's overwhelming you and come back when you feel ready.

> ### *Note from Charlotte*
>
> The psychiatric hospital was the last place I wanted to be, but it was where I finally felt cared for without pressure. That care gave me enough space to stop bracing myself and start breathing again. If you're in a hard season, let others help hold you.

Optional Scripture

"The Lord is close to the brokenhearted and saves those who are crushed in spirit." **Psalm 34:18 (NIV)**

Reflection: Where might God be sheltering you, even when it's hard to feel it?

_____
_____
_____
_____
_____
_____
_____
_____
_____
_____

> ***Faith in the Fog***
>
> God didn't rush me out of crisis. He met me in it. If your healing feels fragile, that's okay. God's love is big enough to hold your breakdowns, your fears, and even your silence. You're still safe with Him.

Reflection Prompt

What has helped you feel emotionally safe, either now or in the past?

_____

_____

_____

_____

_____

_____

_____

What does care (from others or from God) look like in this season?

_____

_____

_____

_____

_____

_____

_____

Optional Facebook Group Prompt

What's one thing you want to remember or return to when you feel overwhelmed or fragile? Share your response in the Lesson 7.2 thread.

Module 7 Resource Box: The Edge of Healing

Want to Go a Little Deeper?

When everything falls apart, it can feel like the end, but sometimes that collapse clears space for truth. This module holds space for surrender, reset, and rebuilding from a more honest place. These resources offer encouragement for those navigating emotional overwhelm and rediscovering safe ground.

Book: *It's Not Supposed to Be This Way* by **Lysa TerKeurst** Written from a place of deep personal sorrow, this book explores what it means to hold on to faith when life breaks open. Raw, real, and grace-filled.

Podcast: *Soul Talks* with **Bill** and **Kristi Gaultiere** **(Episode:** *"When You Feel Emotionally Exhausted"*) Blending psychological insight and spiritual care, this episode offers reassurance and perspective for those feeling worn thin by the healing journey.

Website: *Sanctuary Mental Health Ministries* www.sanctuarymentalhealth.org. Faith-based resources designed to support emotional well-being. Includes downloadable guides and group resources that blend theology and mental health support.

Module 8:

When Coping Breaks Down

Theme Overview
Sometimes, survival looks like slipping back into old patterns just to make it through the day. In this module, we explore what happens when the tools that once helped us cope stop working or even start hurting us. These lessons offer space to grieve the messiness of healing. Notice when you've lost your way and begin again without shame.

Lesson 8.1:
When Fear and Grief Blur the Lines

Lesson Focus
Grief and fear can make it hard to know where we end and where others begin. This lesson explores how anxiety, loneliness, and fear of rejection can lead to blurred emotional boundaries and invites you to reflect on how those patterns may still echo today.

Memoir Vignette
In Chapter 19, after my ex-husband's death, conflicting emotions of grief, fear, and a deep worry that I had failed as a mother overwhelmed me. I wanted to comfort my daughter, but I still struggled to believe I

deserved love or kindness. During this time, I noticed how easily I slipped into unhealthy roles, including over-functioning, appeasing, and doing anything to avoid rejection. These patterns made it hard to recognize what I needed, and even harder to ask for it.

Digging Deeper Activity: Boundary Reflection Tool

Take a deep breath and give yourself a moment to pause. This tool is here to help you name areas where emotional boundaries might feel shaky, especially when you're dealing with intense emotions like grief or fear. As you go through each prompt, take your time and be kind to yourself. Remember, this isn't about judging or blaming; it's an opportunity to reflect, notice patterns that no longer serve you, and think about small, kind steps you can take to move forward with greater clarity and self-care.

When I feel anxious or afraid, I tend to... (e.g., please others, withdraw, take responsibility for others' feelings)

_____

_____

_____

_____

In the past, I've blurred boundaries by... (Saying yes when I meant no, avoiding conflict to feel safe, taking on guilt that didn't belong to me, other...)

_____

_____

_____

_____

One pattern I want to name and gently release is...

_____
_____
_____
_____
_____
_____
_____

A boundary I can begin practicing this week is...

_____
_____
_____
_____
_____
_____
_____

> ### *Note from Charlotte*
>
> I didn't realize how much of my energy was going into keeping people happy. I thought it was love, but it was fear of being left, fear of being wrong. When you notice these patterns, it's not failure, it's awareness, and awareness is a gift.

Optional Scripture

"Am I now trying to win the approval of human beings, or of God?" **Galatians 1:10(NIV)**

Reflection: Where have you traded your voice for someone's approval and what might it mean to reclaim it?

Faith in the Fog

Sometimes God's love feels far away when our boundaries disappear, but He's still near, whispering that your performance or self-sacrifice did not measure your worth. You're allowed to have needs. And He doesn't turn away from them.

Reflection Prompt

When do you feel tempted to ignore your own needs to keep others happy?

What would it look like to stay honest and kind without over-giving?

Optional Facebook Group Prompt

What's one small boundary you're learning to honor in your life and how are you practicing it with care? You're invited to share your response in the Lesson 8.1 thread.

Lesson 8.2: Starting Again with Boundaries

Lesson Focus

This lesson helps you notice where emotional and relational boundaries have broken down and offers a way to rebuild them gently. Even in seasons where everything feels uncertain, you can return to what is yours to hold and release what isn't.

Memoir Vignette

In Chapter 20, I moved back to Lubbock and tried to hold everything together, but I unraveled again. Old habits resurfaced. I acted out, blurred relational lines, and lost touch with the healing I'd worked so hard for. It was painful, but it also helped me realize something important: the path to healing isn't a straight line. I didn't need to be perfect. I just needed to begin again with clearer boundaries and more compassion for myself.

Digging Deeper Activity: My Boundary Rebuild Plan

Sometimes when we use boundaries, we're afraid we'll come across as cold, or maybe we've convinced ourselves that we must fix everything for everyone. But here's the thing: boundaries aren't about shutting people out; they're about making space for your peace while still showing up for others with kindness and care. This worksheet is here to help you figure out what's yours to hold, what you can release, and how to strengthen your boundaries step by step. Take a deep breath, grab a pen, and let's dive in!

Instructions: Take some time to reflect on the emotional and relational boundaries that have felt shaky lately. What situations or patterns keep pulling at your energy?

Use the prompts below to break it down.

Fill in the blanks with what feels true for you right now. Let it be your gentle roadmap to more freedom and peace.

_____
_____
_____
_____
_____
_____
_____
_____

What's Mine to Hold: (My emotions, my healing pace, my choices and responses, other…)

_____
_____
_____
_____
_____
_____
_____
_____
_____
_____
_____

What's Not Mine to Hold: (Other people's reactions, The past, Someone else's growth or pain, other…)

One boundary I want to strengthen this week is:

What might help me strengthen my boundary? (i.e., a phrase I can say: "That's not mine to fix.")

Take your time with this; boundaries are a practice, not a one-time deal. You've got this! (A reminder: "I can be kind without carrying everything.")

> ### *Note from Charlotte*
>
> I used to think boundaries meant pushing people away, but now I see them as a way to love both others and myself well. They help me show up with honesty, not exhaustion. It's okay to start again.

Optional Scripture

"Above all else, guard your heart, for everything you do flows from it." **Proverbs 4:23 (NIV)**

Reflection: What would it mean to guard your heart with grace, not fear?

_____
_____
_____
_____
_____
_____
_____
_____
_____
_____
_____
_____

> ### *Faith in the Fog*
>
> God did not ask me to vanish to be loved. He invites me to live fully with room for my voice, my choices, and my rest. Boundaries aren't barriers, they're invitations to live free.

Reflection Prompt

What's one emotional or relational boundary you've struggled to hold?

How might rebuilding that line help you move forward with more peace?

Optional Facebook Group Prompt

Share a phrase, reminder, or practice that's helping you hold healthier boundaries this week. You're invited to share your response in the Lesson 8.2 thread.

Module 8 Resource Box: When Coping Breaks Down

Want to Go a Little Deeper?

It's painful to realize that what once helped us survive is now holding us back. This module creates space to notice old coping strategies with compassion and to begin again without shame. These resources offer insight into boundaries, emotional patterns, and how to reconnect with what's healthy and true.

Book: *Boundaries* by **Dr. Henry Cloud & Dr. John Townsend**
A classic, faith-based guide to understanding where you end and others begin. Especially helpful for those who tend to over-function, people-please, or lose themselves in relationships.

Podcast: *Therapy & Theology* with **Lysa TerKeurst** (**Episode:** "Am I Codependent or Just Being Loving?") This episode explores emotional boundaries in a grace-filled way and helps listeners discern the difference between love and self-neglect.

Website: *Darlene Lancer*– **Codependency Resources** www.whatiscodependency.com Includes articles, tools, and quizzes to help you understand patterns of over-responsibility and start reclaiming your voice.

Module 9:

Shame, Self-Worth, and the First Glimpse of Grace

Theme Overview

Shame can convince us we're too broken to be loved. It isolates, distorts, and whispers that we've gone too far. But shame isn't the end of the story. In this module, we name the weight of shame and the lies it tells, and we also notice the quiet ways grace shows up. Those who love us unconditionally find us lovable, regardless of our actions. Sometimes it comes as a whisper from God that says, "You're still mine." This is where the story turns, not with perfection, but with possibility.

Lesson 9.1:
The Weight of Shame

Lesson Focus

This lesson explores the emotional toll of shame and self-loathing. We will consider how shame shapes our beliefs about God, ourselves, and love, and begin to challenge them.

Memoir Vignette

In Chapter 21, I emotionally unraveled. I began acting out again, driven by confusion, shame, and a deep belief that I had disappointed God beyond repair. I believed my brokenness was beyond repair, and that God hated me for it. Overwhelming shame consumed me, not just for my actions, but also because I doubted my lovability.

Digging Deeper Activity: Naming Shame's Voice

Let's pause for a second and recognize how sneaky shame can be. It sneaks in and plants seeds of doubt about our worth, whispering lies that feel so loud we believe them. But here's the thing: shame thrives when it's unnamed. That's why this activity is all about shining a light on the voice of shame and challenging it with truth.

The goal is not to "fix" anything or to prove anything. It's just about noticing the messages shame has tried to feed you and stepping into a space where you can hold those lies up to the truth.

Step 1: Think about one specific message shame has tried to tell you about yourself. Write it down:

_____
_____
_____
_____
_____
_____

Step 2: Reflect on how that message feels or sounds. Does it remind you of a certain voice, a specific memory, or maybe just a heavy feeling? Write what comes up:

_____
_____
_____
_____
_____

Step 3: Consider which part of you might believe that message. Is it a younger version of yourself? Which part of you is hurt? Or maybe the part of you that feels afraid? Note it:

_____
_____
_____
_____
_____

Step 4: Now, take a breath and think about the truth you'd like to speak back to that voice. What would you say if you could challenge that lie today? Write it down:

_____
_____
_____
_____
_____

There's no "wrong" way to do this. What matters is that you're showing up and being honest with yourself. Each step you take here is a step toward reclaiming your voice and silencing the shame.

> ### Note from Charlotte
>
> Shame made me believe I had to earn love, and that I had already failed. But healing began when I stopped trying to prove my worth and just let the ache be real. If shame traps you, know that you are not alone. Just know this: shame lies, and healing begins when we start to listen to a different voice.

Optional Scripture

"Therefore, there is now no condemnation for those who are in Christ Jesus." **Romans 8:1 (NIV)**

Reflection: What's the difference between conviction and condemnation?

_____

_____

_____

_____

_____

_____

_____

_____

_____

_____

_____

Which voice have you been listening to?

> ### *Faith in the Fog*
>
> God didn't walk away from me in that season, though I thought He had. He stayed near, even when I couldn't feel it. Shame says we're abandoned. Grace says we're held.

Reflection Prompt

What message has shame tried to root into your identity?

What truth might replace it, even if it feels hard to believe right now?

Optional Facebook Group Prompt

Without sharing anything too personal, what's one truth you want to hold on to when shame speaks? You're invited to share your response in the Lesson 9.1 thread.

Lesson 9.2:
Love That Doesn't Have to Be Earned

Lesson Focus

This lesson explores the shift from performance-based love to receiving grace. We reflect on the first signs that love might be real, even when we're at our worst.

Memoir Vignette

The end of Chapter 21 marked a turning point. I returned to church and met the singles' pastors whose love and presence felt radically different from what I'd known. There were no strings, no judgment, just consistent kindness and in that space, I believed that maybe, just maybe, God still loved me. It didn't fix everything, but it opened the door to something new: the possibility of grace I didn't have to earn.

Digging Deeper Activity: Signs of Unconditional Love

How about we pause for a second to think about what it really means to experience unconditional love? It's not always flashy or dramatic; it can show up in small, quiet ways that surprise us. Sometimes, we don't even recognize it until we look back. This activity is meant to help you notice those moments and consider what they might be trying to tell you about the kind of love that's always been there for you, with no strings attached.

Here's how to get started: Think about times in your life when someone showed you kindness or acceptance, especially when you felt the least deserving of it. These might be big gestures or simple actions that touched your heart.

Use the prompts below to guide your thoughts. Feel free to jot them down or simply think them through, whatever works best for you!

Someone showed me kindness when I didn't feel I deserved it. That looked like:

_____
_____
_____

A moment I felt seen or accepted was:

_____
_____
_____

What made that moment feel different?

_____
_____
_____

What does this tell me about the kind of love I need more of?

_____
_____
_____

> ### *Note from Charlotte*
>
> The singles pastors didn't try to fix me. They listened. They stayed and in doing so they showed me a picture of love I hadn't seen before. Sometimes God speaks loudest through people who just keep showing up.

Optional Scripture

1 John 4:10 "This is love: not that we loved God, but that he loved us..." **(NIV)**

Reflection: What does it stir in you to imagine that God's love comes first, not last?

Faith in the Fog

When you've lived most of your life trying to earn love, grace feels suspicious. But God's love doesn't ask for performance. We've already received it. You're already His.

Reflection Prompt

Where have you seen glimpses of unconditional love?

What might change if you believed that love could include you?

Optional Facebook Group Prompt

What does 'unearned love' look like to you and how are you learning to trust it? You're invited to share your response in the Lesson 9.2 thread.

Module 9 Resource Box: Shame, Self-Worth, and the First Glimpse of Grace

Want to Go a Little Deeper?

Shame says, "You are too much or not enough." But grace whispers a different story. This module invites you to name the lies shame has told you and begin practicing a new way of seeing yourself. These resources offer both compassion and clarity for that shift.

Book: *Shame Interrupted* by **Ed Welch**

A Christ-centered guide to understanding shame and how God meets us in the middle of it, not with condemnation, but with love and restoration.

Podcast: *The Place We Find Ourselves* with Adam Young (**Episode:** *"What Is the Voice of Shame?"*) This episode explores how shame sounds and feels and how we can begin to distinguish it from truth. Especially helpful for naming internal messages that keep us stuck.

Website: Soul Shepherding–**Grace-Focused Devotionals and Tools**
www.soulshepherding.org This site blends emotional health and spiritual formation. Their devotionals and soul care tools offer reminders that you are deeply loved, no matter what shame says.

Module 10:

Integration, Grace, and Moving Forward

Theme Overview

Healing isn't about perfection; it's about learning to live with more grace, more honesty, and more truth. In this final module, we reflect on what it looks like to use the tools we've gathered along the way and to move forward with faith and care. Even when we fall back into old patterns, there is space to begin again. These lessons explore how to stay grounded, trust grace, and carry what you've learned into everyday life.

Lesson 10.1:
Tools That Help Us Stay Grounded

Lesson Focus

This lesson explores how we heal by replacing old patterns with new tools. Even when shame and confusion feel overwhelming, we can learn to respond with grace instead of fear.

Memoir Vignette

Following my breakup with Johnny, described in Chapter 22, I suffered an emotional decline and relapsed into old patterns. I felt unworthy, lost, and overwhelmed. However, during the same season, I began developing tools that would eventually help me stay grounded. With the consistent support of the singles pastors, I blended what I knew about trauma with what I believed about God. These weren't formal lessons yet, they were survival strategies that became lifelong healing practices.

Digging Deeper Activity: Using the Relate Journal

This journaling tool became part of my healing when I needed to sort through emotional overwhelm without spiraling. It helped me calm the chaos, stay grounded, and gently bring God's truth into the moment. I still use the Relate Journal when something triggers powerful emotions.

This process, adapted from *The Relate Journal*, originates from work I developed and later shared with trusted colleagues in 2016. The Relate Program now includes it, and we use it here with permission. A printed version is available for purchase through their ministry >>>Relate Journal. You can also download a free sample of the journal here.

If you've ever felt shame or confusion are taking over, this tool can help you slow down, name what's happening, and reconnect with what's true.

Step 1: Review–What Happened? *(Trigger)*

What happened right before your emotions became intense? Keep it brief—one or two sentences

"I got an email from my boss…"
"My child didn't respond the way I expected…"

Step 2: Reveal–What Did I Think and Feel? *(Emotional Response)*

Name your feelings or thoughts. Again, keep it simple—just a word or a short phrase.

"Disrespected."
"Alone."
"Ashamed."

Step 3: Regroup—What Kind of Connection Do I Need? *(Focus)*

What would help soothe your emotions at this moment? Connection with a friend, quiet time with God, movement, prayer?

"Gentle reassurance."
"Worship music."
"Physical space."

Step 4: Rehearse—What Does God's Word Say? *(God's Solution)*

Pick a scripture that aligns with what you need. Speak it aloud. Write it down. Then read it aloud again

The Lord is close to the brokenhearted…" **Psalm 34:18 (NIV)**

Step 5: Reclaim–What Is the Truth? *(Declaration)*

Write a few truths based on what you've just experienced. Let them anchor you.

Note from Charlotte

The first time I used this journaling tool, I was in a crisis. I needed something to slow my thoughts down. It didn't fix everything, but it helped me breathe. Over time, I started to trust that I didn't have to figure everything out in the moment; I just had to take the next right step.

Optional Scripture

"In repentance and rest is your salvation, in quietness and trust is your strength…" **Isaiah 30:15 (NIV)**

Reflection: What helps you return to quietness and trust when you feel overwhelmed?

> **_Faith in the Fog_**
>
> Sometimes our tools are prayers. Sometimes they're pens. Either way, God meets us in that moment, not with shame, but with presence.

Reflection Prompt

What's one moment when a tool helped you stay present instead of spiraling?

How can you build more pauses into your healing rhythm?

Optional Facebook Group Prompt

If you've used *TheRelate Journal* or another grounding practice recently, how did it help you pause or find clarity? You're invited to share your response in the Lesson 10.1 thread.

Lesson 10.2:
Living What You've Learned

Lesson Focus

Healing is never about perfection; rather, it's about choosing honesty, accountability, and grace day by day. This lesson reflects on what it means to practice the tools, extend grace to yourself, and step into new relationships from a place of truth.

Memoir Vignette

In Chapters 23 and 24, the singles pastors continued to support me with kindness and truth. I began to help others using the same tools that had helped me. My relationship with my daughter healed, and when Johnny and I eventually reconnected and married, it was different, healthier, slower, grounded in honesty. Even after his death, I didn't spiral. I had learned enough to carry myself forward. That's what healing gave me: not a perfect life, but a more anchored one.

Digging Deeper Activity: What Healing Looks Like Now

Healing is a journey, not a destination; it's a process that unfolds day by day. Sometimes, it can feel like you're taking leaps forward; other times, healing is as subtle as finding a small moment of clarity or choosing grace for yourself. This activity is here to help you pause, reflect, and honor where you are right now. Don't worry about making it perfect, just be honest with yourself as you explore these prompts.

Here's how you can dive in:

Take a few minutes to sit in a quiet space or wherever you feel most comfortable.

Think about the tools and practices that have supported you, the ways you've grown, and the areas where you're still learning.

Answer each question below as fully or as briefly as you like. You can write, speak, or even just meditate on your responses; it's all about what works for you.

Try these prompts as a guide:

A tool or practice that still helps me is:

_____
_____
_____
_____
_____
_____
_____

One way I've grown emotionally or spiritually is:

_____
_____
_____
_____
_____
_____
_____
_____

Faith In The Fog

Something I'm still working on (and that's okay):

In moving forward, I intend to:

> ### *Note from Charlotte*
>
> Healing doesn't mean you'll never struggle again. It means you know how to be honest with yourself when you do. It means you know what helps, and you give yourself permission to use it.

Optional Scripture

"He who began a good work in you will carry it on to completion..." **Philippians 1:6 (NIV)**

Reflection: What is God still carrying in you that you don't have to finish alone?

_____
_____
_____
_____
_____
_____
_____
_____
_____
_____
_____
_____

> ### *Faith in the Fog*
>
> Grace doesn't always look like a breakthrough. Sometimes it's as quiet as getting out of bed, telling the truth, or showing up anyway. That's holy, too.

Reflection Prompt

What does healing look like for you right now?

What are you learning to accept—and celebrate—about your journey?

Optional Facebook Group Prompt

As we finish this workbook, what's one truth or tool you're carrying with you into the next season? You're invited to share your response in the Lesson 10.2 thread.

Module 10 Resource Box: Integration, Grace, and Moving Forward

Want to Go a Little Deeper?

Healing isn't about crossing a finish line; it's about learning to live with more honesty, grace, and resilience. This final module celebrates your progress and offers encouragement to keep practicing what you've learned. These resources support ongoing reflection, spiritual integration, and staying grounded when life gets hard again.

Book: *Emotionally Healthy Spirituality* by **Pete Scazzero**

This book explores how spiritual maturity and emotional health are deeply connected—and why we can't grow in one area while ignoring the other. A helpful guide for building long-term wholeness.

Podcast: *The Next Right Thing* by **Emily P. Freeman** (**Episode:** *"Let the Listener Decide"*) A gentle, contemplative reminder that your story matters and you don't have to explain or fix everything. A perfect send-off for this season of your journey.

Website: Soul Care Institute
www.soulcareinstitute.com
Offers long-term formation opportunities, but also includes blogs and articles on spiritual rhythms, emotional honesty, and sustainable healing. A good place to explore if you want to keep growing at a soul-deep pace.

Appendices

Appendix A: Glossary of Terms

This glossary is here to help you feel more at ease with the words and ideas you'll see throughout the workbook. These definitions aren't clinical; they're intended to support your understanding and give you language for what may have once felt too hard to name.

Attachment
The bond we form with caregivers early in life. These relationships shape how we connect with others and ourselves later.

Body Memory
A physical sensation that holds emotional weight, even when we don't remember why. Our bodies sometimes "remember" what our minds have blocked out.

Boundaries
The emotional, physical, and relational lines that help define what's ours to carry and what's not. Boundaries protect connection, not prevent it.

Coping Strategy
Anything we do, consciously or not, to manage stress, pain, or fear. Some are healthy. Some helped us survive but now need to be replaced.

Dissociation
A feeling of disconnection from your body, emotions, or surroundings. Often a protective response when something feels too overwhelming to fully process.

Dissociative Amnesia

A survival response where the brain blocks out painful or traumatic memories. This kind of forgetting often happens in childhood trauma and can last for years. The body may still hold the memory even when the mind does not.

Flashback

When an experience (or parts of it) suddenly feels present again through emotions, body sensations, or mental images. Flashbacks aren't always visual.

Grounding

A way to come back to the present moment, especially when you feel overwhelmed. Grounding helps you reconnect with safety and awareness in the "now."

Inner Child

The younger parts of you that still hold memories, emotions, or unmet needs. Connecting with those parts gently can be part of the healing process.

Performance-Based Love

The belief that love must be earned by doing things "right." This often stems from childhood experiences where love felt conditional.

Relational Trauma

Wounding that happens in relationships, especially those that should have been safe often leads to shame, confusion, and trust struggles.

Shame

The belief that something is wrong with you, not just that you've done something wrong. Shame often says, "I'm not enough," or "I'm too much."

Survival Mode

The state of doing whatever it takes to get through, often by shutting down emotions, staying hyper-alert, or pleasing others at your own expense.

Trigger

Something that brings up a strong emotional, physical, or mental response because it reminds your body or mind of past pain.

Appendix B:
Tools and Worksheets Index

This index includes all the Digging Deeper activities from the Faith in the Fog workbook, organized by module and lesson. Each activity offered gentle, trauma-informed support as you explore your story. You are welcome to revisit them at any time, and printable versions of many tools are available at:

charlottethomason.com/downloads

Tool Title	Purpose	Module & Lesson
Love Map	Explore past beliefs about love through words, images, or feelings.	Module 1, Lesson 1.1
Replacing Old Beliefs	Name internalized messages and practice new, healing truths.	Module 1, Lesson 1.2
Safe or Small	Reflect on moments when staying small felt safer than being seen.	Module 2, Lesson 2.1
Sorting the Unspoken	Name confusing childhood experiences and what you needed at the time.	Module 2, Lesson 2.2
Anchors in the Storm	Recall moments of peace or divine comfort in the middle of fear.	Module 3, Lesson 3.1

Tool Title	Purpose	Module & Lesson
Trust Checkpoints	Reflect on early glimpses of safety and what made them feel different.	Module 3, Lesson 3.2
What Holding It Together Looks Like	Examine the gap between how you appear and what's happening inside.	Module 4, Lesson 4.1
Grace Moments List	Name small experiences of grace or comfort that helped you hold on.	Module 4, Lesson 4.2
Holding Two Truths	Explore the tension between joy and pain in moments that shaped you.	Module 5, Lesson 5.1
What Silence Protected	Reflect on how denial, silence, or withdrawal helped you survive.	Module 5, Lesson 5.2
Grounding When Triggered	Use a simple object + questions to reconnect with safety during overwhelm.	Module 6, Lesson 6.1

Tool Title	Purpose	Module & Lesson
My Healing Pace Check-In	Assess whether you're rushing or honoring your emotional rhythm.	Module 6, Lesson 6.2
Naming the Ruins	Gently acknowledge what has come undone—and what it might make space for.	Module 7, Lesson 7.1
Self-Care in Crisis Plan	Build a simple, personalized plan to stay grounded during emotional spikes.	Module 7, Lesson 7.2
Boundary Reflection Tool	Name emotional patterns and gently reclaim your needs.	Module 8, Lesson 8.1
My Boundary Rebuild Plan	Clarify what's yours to hold and where to draw compassionate lines.	Module 8, Lesson 8.2
Naming Shame's Voice	Name how shame speaks—and begin replacing it with truth.	Module 9, Lesson 9.1

Tool Title	Purpose	Module & Lesson
My Healing Pace Check-In	Assess whether you're rushing or honoring your emotional rhythm.	Module 6, Lesson 6.2
Signs of Unconditional Love	Reflect on moments when you received love you didn't think you deserved.	Module 9, Lesson 9.2
The Relate Journal (Abbreviated)	Process triggers and emotions through a structured 5-step journaling tool	Module 10, Lesson 10.1
What Healing Looks Like Now	Celebrating growth, name current supports, and reflect on future steps.	Module 10, Lesson 10.2

Appendix C: Additional Resources

This list brings together books, podcasts, and websites that support the healing journey—spiritually, emotionally, and practically. I mentioned some in earlier modules, while others come from my library of trusted resources. You don't need to explore everything; just begin with what feels helpful for where you are right now.

Books for Healing and Recovery

- *Permission to Feel* by **Marc Brackett** A helpful, research-based book that teaches you how to recognize, name, and work with your emotions. Especially useful if you've spent years shutting feelings down.

- *Mother Hunger* by **Kelly McDaniel** Written for women who missed nurturing early in life, this book unpacks the ache for connection and how it can shape adulthood.

- *The Body Keeps the Score* by **Bessel van der Kolk** A trauma classic that explains how the body holds onto trauma even when the mind forgets. Dense but powerful—read at your own pace.

- *Emotionally Healthy Spirituality* by **Pete Scazzero** Explores the connection between spiritual maturity and emotional healing. Offers tools for faith-based self-awareness and growth.

- *It's Not Supposed to Be This Way* by **Lysa TerKeurst** A faith-filled reflection on loss, confusion, and holding on to God when life falls apart. Gentle and relatable.

Faith-Based Encouragement

- *The Soul of Shame* by **Curt Thompson** Explores how shame distorts our relationships and how God invites us into healing through being seen, known, and loved.

- *Shame Interrupted* by **Ed Welch** A grace-centered look at how shame affects our lives and how Scripture speaks a better truth.

- *Safe People* by **Henry Cloud & John Townsend** Helps you understand who is emotionally safe to let into your life—and how to set healthy boundaries in relationships.

Podcasts and Audio Resources

- **The Next Right Thing with Emily P. Freeman** Short, reflective episodes that help you slow down and listen for God's voice. Perfect for quiet mornings or uncertain seasons.

- **Unspoken: Stories of Trauma and Healing** Real people share their stories of pain, healing, and hope. Encouraging for those who feel alone on their journey.

- **Grace for the Journey** A soft, Scripture-rooted podcast that offers bite-sized encouragement when life feels heavy.

- **Soul Talks with Bill & Kristi Gaultiere** Blends psychological insight with spiritual care. Ideal for those looking for honest, faith-informed healing.

- **Therapy & Theology with Lysa TerKeurst** Explores emotional health and faith through personal stories and professional insights. Grace-filled and accessible.

Websites and Downloadable Tools

- **The Allender Center**

https://www.theallendercenter.org Focused on story-based healing and trauma recovery. Includes blogs, courses, and podcast episodes.

- **Grace Alliance**

https://www.mentalhealthgracealliance.org Faith-based resources for mental health support. Offers small group guides and recovery tools.

- **Sanctuary Mental Health Ministries**

https://www.sanctuarymentalhealth.org Integrates mental health awareness with spiritual formation. Ideal for churches and small groups.

- **Darlene Lancer–Codependency Tools**

https://www.whatiscodependency.com Simple tools for recognizing and recovering from codependent patterns.

- **Soul Shepherding**

https://www.soulshepherding.org Faith-based devotionals and spiritual direction resources. Gentle, practical, and soul-nourishing.

- **The Attachment Project**

https://www.attachmentproject.com Provides quizzes, articles, and accessible science on how early attachment shapes adult relationships.

On My Website

You can explore even more curated resources at: https://charlottethomason.com/suggested-resources This page includes trusted podcasts, books, healing programs, and online tools, plus links to anything new that I may recommend in the future.

Appendix D: Small Group Guide

If you're walking through this workbook with others, thank you. Whether you're leading a small group, a church class, or simply gathering with a few trusted friends, creating a space for honest conversation is a beautiful act of courage and care.

This guide is here to support you as you offer a space of reflection, safety, and connection. It's not about being an expert; it's about listening well, going slow, and honoring each person's pace. Healing doesn't happen in a straight line, and it's not something we rush. This group doesn't need to "fix" anything. It's here to make space for reflection, safety, and presence.

Creating a Safe and Respectful Space

- Honor each person's pace. Some participants may speak freely. Others may need silence and time. Both are welcome.

- Let the story belong to the person sharing it. There's no need to explain, correct, or interpret someone else's experience.

- No one must share. You can learn and grow just by listening.

- Confidentiality matters. What's shared in the group stays in the group.

- Avoid spiritual bypassing. Sometimes people need to sit with a hard question—not jump straight to a solution.

- Be mindful of group time. Encourage everyone to share, but also to leave room for others. If someone speaks at length or drifts off-topic, it's okay for the leader to gently and kindly redirect the conversation with clarity.

Suggested Pacing

This workbook includes 10 modules, each with two lessons. You can move through them:

- Weekly (1 lesson per week)

- Bi-weekly (1 module every 2 weeks)

- Or at your own pace, depending on the needs of your group

Encourage group members to engage with the Digging Deeper activities and reflections between meetings. But always remind them: there's no "behind." There's just the next step.

Sample Discussion Prompts

Here are a few gentle questions to support meaningful conversation:

- What stood out to you in this week's reading or reflection?

- Did anything surprise you, feel familiar, or make you pause?

- Was there a tool or activity that helped you notice something about yourself?

- Did anything feel uncomfortable or confused and what might that mean?

- How are you experiencing God on this part of the journey?

You can also borrow from the Facebook group prompts at the end of each lesson, or simply ask: "What would you like to share today?"

Appendix E:
A Note for Counselors, Pastors, and Support People

If you're a counselor, pastor, mentor, or support person using this workbook alongside someone else, thank you for the work you do. You already bring knowledge, insight, and deep care into the spaces you hold—and I hope that this resource can complement the support you're offering.

Faith in the Fog is a companion to my memoir, *What Kind of Love Is This?* which tells my personal story of trauma, survival, and faith. While the memoir shares the journey through the lens of lived experience, this workbook offers tools that may help others as they explore their own stories. Reading the memoir is not required to use the workbook because each lesson stands on its own and offers reflection and support regardless of familiarity with my story.

This resource is not a clinical manual, nor is it a devotional. It's something in between: a trauma-informed, faith-rooted guide designed to foster reflection, emotional regulation, and spiritual engagement.

You may find this workbook helpful in several ways:

• As a structured companion for clients or group members already in counseling or spiritual formation work.

• As a guided journaling or reflection tool for individuals working through trauma, faith deconstruction, or identity questions.

• As a resource for gently inviting deeper emotional awareness in ministry, mentoring, or pastoral care settings.

Each module includes reflection activities, emotional tools, and optional prompts for group discussion or spiritual exploration. While written for survivors of childhood trauma, many find this resource relevant to a wide range of experiences, including grief, betrayal, loss, spiritual confusion, and the slow work of restoration.

If you're using this with a group or one-on-one, Appendix D provides practical suggestions for creating a space of respect and safety.

We do not intend this workbook to replace therapy or crisis care. If you notice someone becoming emotionally overwhelmed or stuck in a trauma response, your encouragement to seek clinical support may be the most compassionate next step.

Thank you for making space for stories. For presence. For listening. That work is sacred.

Appendix F:
About the Author

Charlotte B. Thomason is a writer, speaker, and trauma survivor who has spent over 35 years mentoring others through emotional and spiritual recovery. With an MSW and an MA in Christian Apologetics, she blends professional insight with personal experience to create trauma-informed, faith-rooted resources for healing.

Her memoir, *What Kind of Love Is This?* tells the story of a little girl's search for love and belonging through the lens of childhood trauma, faith, and survival. This workbook, *Faith in the Fog*, comes from the same story, but is written for your story.

Charlotte's passion is helping others feel less alone in their pain, especially those who carry shame or spiritual confusion rooted in early wounding. She speaks with honesty, gentleness, and hope, inviting people to move at their own pace, to listen to their younger selves, and to rediscover the God who never stopped loving them.

She lives in Texas near her family and enjoys painting, reading, and playing Minecraft, often while thinking about her next story. You can find more of her writing, videos, and resources at:
www.charlottethomason.com

Appendix G:
Stay Connected

One should never walk the healing journey alone. If this workbook has encouraged you, challenged you, or simply helped you feel seen, I'd love to stay in touch.

Whether you're looking for more tools, a sense of community, or the next step on your journey, here are a few ways we can keep walking together:

Visit my website

You'll find articles, videos, podcast interviews, and other free resources at:
www.charlottethomason.com

Explore the companion course

If you'd like to take this work deeper, there's an online course that walks through the same material, complete with videos, guided prompts, and group discussion options.

Download more tools

The Digging Deeper tools and bonus worksheets are available for free on my Downloads page:
www.charlottethomason.com/downloads

Join the conversation

Each course has an optional private Facebook group, introduced through the Dialogue Zone. You can learn more and find links at:
www.charlottethomason.com/forum

Share your story or feedback

If you'd like to tell me what stood out to you—or if you have suggestions or a story to share—I'd love to hear from you.

There's a contact form on the website, or you can reach out directly at:
charlotte@charlottethomason.com

Thank you for trusting me to walk this road with you. I'm so glad you're here.

Other Books by the Author

What Kind of Love Is This?

A memoir about trauma, survival, and finding God in the darkness. Told through the eyes of a child, this honest and hope-filled story invites readers to step into healing at their own pace.

Light in the Darkness: 25 Devotionals for Trauma Survivors

A gentle devotional companion for those walking through grief, confusion, or early recovery. Rooted in Scripture and personal reflection, these daily readings offer encouragement for weary hearts.

For more details, visit:
www.charlottethomason.com/books-hub

About
Kharis Publishing

Kharis Publishing, an imprint of Kharis Media LLC, is a leading Christian and inspirational book publisher based in Aurora, Chicago metropolitan area, Illinois. Kharis' dual mission is to give voice to under-represented writers (including women and first-time authors) and equip orphans in developing countries with literacy tools. That is why, for each book sold, the publisher channels some of the proceeds into providing books and computers for orphanages in developing countries so that these kids may learn to read, dream, and grow. For a limited time, Kharis Publishing is accepting unsolicited queries for nonfiction (Christian, self-help, memoirs, business, health and wellness) from qualified leaders, professionals, pastors, and ministers. Learn more at: https://kharispublishing.com/

www.ingramcontent.com/pod-product-compliance
Lightning Source LLC
Chambersburg PA
CBHW070154100426
42743CB00013B/2910